"This information packed volume provides ten simple step by step lessons parents can easily use to supplement their child's reading program. It's concise nature should appeal to parents who want to avoid jargon and adopt a quick, easy approach to home tutoring needs."

The Midwest Book Review

"Joyce Corbin gives parents sage advice when she says their number one task is to read and write themselves. When children see the importance of literacy in their parents' lives, they don't want to be left out."

Dr. Jane Hansen, Professor
Education Department
University of New Hampshire

"Your book was loaned to me by a veteran special needs educator in my school. What a find! I had been planning to start a parent-school partnership around my second grade early intervention reading program, and I had been searching for a straight-forward, compact, and user-friendly book to give to my parents. Your book is a quick read, with summary pages at the end of each chapter to assist parents who have only a few minutes to understand what is being suggested."

Barbara Roberts
Reading Specialist

"Thank you so much for your wonderful book. We found it very easy to follow and understand. Our seven year old son has benefited greatly from your techniques and I can't wait to try it on my two year old daughter."

Jennifer Suprino
Home Schooler

Reading
Success
For
Children

Reading Success For Children

What Every Parent Should Know

Joyce Corbin, M.Ed.

Learning Strategies
Rye Beach, NH

Quantity discounts are available for bulk purchase for educational, business, or sales promotional uses.

Cover illustration by Debbie McConnell.

Please visit our website: helpkidsread.com

Publisher's Cataloging in Publication
(Prepared by Quality Books, Inc.)

Corbin, Joyce.
    Reading success for children: what every parent should know / Joyce Corbin.
    p. cm.
    Includes bibliographical references and index.
    ISBN 0-9630773-0-9

    1. reading __ Parent participation __ Guide books.
I. Title.

LB1050   372.41

                                    QBI91 - 1395
                                    91-75990

This book is dedicated to my husband, Ernest who has talked to me about reading and children for the last twenty years. He tells me that his reading skills have improved from reading and critiquing this book. This book is as much his as it is mine. Thank you, E.C.

The gender changes from chapter to chapter are intended. The reason for this is to emphasize that all children need parental support, not just boys or just girls. To avoid awkward statements using he/she, the gender of "the child" alternates from chapter to chapter.

TABLE OF CONTENTS

The Reason

Failure to learn to read at the beginning of a child's school career invariably results in school and life failure. This is a strong statement, but after fifteen years as a classroom teacher and Reading Specialist, I have found this to be true.

There are school programs designed to make up for early failure and some of them are successful. Many of them are not. The only way to guarantee success for your children is to participate in teaching them to read before starting school and during the school years.

This book is for parents who want their children to learn to read and write, do well in school, get a good job and be happy. I first thought of writing this book after many parents had said to me, "I'd like to help my child with reading but I don't know what to do". I would meet with them to teach them what has ended up being the information in this book. They were able to help their children become more successful in school by consistently following this step by step plan.

This plan makes beginning reading and writing easy and fun. Parents find that these strategies become so natural that they are always helping their children to think and be successful without even trying!

There is no greater joy in the world than seeing the look of pride on the face of a child who has just read a book to you. You can share that pride of accomplishment when you read with your child.

THE INTRODUCTION

The Beginning

It is a widely accepted belief in education that students whose parents help them to prepare for school are much more successful than those students whose parents sit them in front of a television set day after day.

Television watching is part of our culture. I am not condemning television. I am promoting taking 15-30 minutes a day to prepare your children for school. During this time you will begin by talking to your children about the world around them and their experiences. This will build the language base. If children are not able to use and understand the language of their world, they can not learn to read and write.

Next you will work with them to begin to learn to read and write. During this 15-30 minute period of daily time you can begin to develop and build literacy skills that will set the framework for further education.

I have successfully used the strategies described in this volume with many students. You can provide the most valuable, long-lasting experiences of your child's life by following the steps in this book.

The best way to use this book is to read it all of the way through at least once, to become familiar with the steps. At the end of each chapter, there are questions for you to think about to help you organize the new information. Do not worry about doing the wrong thing. As long as you do not criticize your child, no harm can be done. When you feel comfortable with a chapter, add that step to your reading activities. After a few sessions this will be quite natural. The strategies described in this book will make your reading time together a powerful and successful experience.

You will find that it takes only 15 to 30 minutes a day to help your child learn to read. The time you spend reading and learning together will be a time for you to build your child's self-esteem and skills. Your interest, encouragement and time will greatly increase your child's opportunity for school and life success.

Before reading any further, think about the following questions and jot down your answers. Re-read these questions when you have finished the book and see how your answers have changed.

- How did you learn to read?

- How do children learn to read?

- Write down all of the words that you can think of that are related to learning to read.

- Now look over this book. What do you think you will learn?

Summary

1) Children learn from their parents that reading is important.

2) There are easy strategies that parents can use every day to help their children become successful.

3) It only takes 15 to 30 minutes a day to teach your child to read.

Happy reading!

CHAPTER ONE

Literacy Modeling

"Monkey See, Monkey Do"

The most important thing that you can do to help your child become literate is to read and write yourself. You can begin this very simply by reading when you are with your child. Just ten minutes a day is enough in the beginning.

There are many ways to bring reading into your daily life. Reading road signs, menus, boxes, grocery items, bags, cookbooks, magazines, mail, and sales fliers, out loud together shows that being able to read is important. Another example is to read aloud from the newspaper, and then ask your children what they think about the news. These reading activities can be done while you are doing other things. They are also important to develop a good vocabulary.

You can write your child notes and ask him to write back or you can have a family message board. A family message board can be the refrigerator or a bulletin board located in a place where everyone in the family can reach it. The purpose is to send messages to each other. They could be phone messages, chores, happy notes, secret surprises or anything else that practices reading and writing.

These activities all share the purpose of getting and giving information. Modeling (showing by example) that reading has a purpose in life, as well as in school, will encourage your child to use reading daily.

At the same time you need to think about getting books and magazines into your home. One way to do this is to join the public library. Set a time every two weeks to visit the library with your children and family members, including grandparents, if possible. You can make your selections in 30 minutes or less. Help your child choose books with a variety of topics and levels of reading difficulty. Some of them you will read to your child. Some he will read, and some you will read together. The children's librarian can help you. After a few visits you will probably have found a few favorites that you will want to buy to begin your home library. In soft cover many children's books are under five dollars. Encourage your friends and family to give books as gifts. Exchanging books with friends is another way to enlarge your library. It is really nice to have old favorites to pass on through the family. In this way you can begin to build your child's personal library.

Remember that children learn what is valuable by what their parents value. If you spend time and money on this venture, your child will learn to value it also.

Once you have established a daily routine for reading time, and you have started building a home library, you are ready to try the other steps in this book.

Remember, whenever you are working with your child on reading and writing, you need to be extremely careful not to criticize. Learning to read and write is risky business for all of us. Children can become discouraged very easily. I have had students as young as six years old tell me that they were stupid because they had not yet learned to read.

Parents and teachers need to listen to the way they speak to children. Never tell your child that he is stupid or not as good as a brother or sister. Don't even say these things about your child to someone else. Children are very perceptive. Even if you don't actually say negative things to the child but you act impatiently or disgustedly, your child will know that you think he is inadequate.

When you are reading to your child encourage him to guess at the meanings of new words, or what will happen next in the story. Encourage all answers. Find all that is "right" about the answer he tells you.

For example if your child guesses "window" for "door" as you're reading, say "It could be a window because you can go in and out of it, but what else can you go in and out of that starts with 'd' or the sound 'd-d-d-'." Keep giving clues until he can guess the word. If you find that he can't get the word say, "Maybe this word is a little too hard right now, we'll try another one." Always give them 5-10 seconds to try to figure it out. Whenever one of my students makes an error I always tell him that I am glad to see that there is something that I can teach him.

Timing is very important when working on reading. Frequently parents expect children to read like little adults, and learn new information as quickly as we do. This is simply not the case. If you are presenting new information to your child, information that you already know, you cannot expect him to learn and use the new ideas as quickly as you can.

Try to think of a time that you were trying to learn a new skill and how vulnerable you felt. I always tell my students of my continuing efforts to learn how to play tennis, despite the many times I've run right into the ball, head first. I relate how embarrassed I felt and how much I dislike it when my friends laugh at me. Well, many children feel that way about reading. You don't want your child to feel that way about reading. You need to allow your child to feel that he can trust you not to laugh at him or criticize him.

You <u>must</u> make positive comments all during the reading time. Some of my favorites are: "Good guess!", "Almost, you got the first part of the word", "Excellent!", etc. You must remember that for a child learning to read, knowing one word more today than yesterday is an important accomplishment. You might say, "I can tell that you are really trying to remember these words, good job." Always notice and comment positively on small improvements. You can comment on smoothness of reading, expression in the voice, correction of his own mistakes and anything else that you notice that shows progress.

The following chapters teach you how to get your child ready to read.

Summary

1) Children learn that reading is important from their parents.

2) If parents value reading, their children will too.

3) Read to your child.

4) Make reading part of the daily routine.

5) Join the local library.

6) Build a home library.

7) BE POSITIVE.

8) DO NOT CRITICIZE.

Was the information in this chapter what you guessed it would be? Close your eyes and see how many of the items from this list you can remember.

Thinking about everything you've read so far, what do you think the next chapter will be about? Read on and find out.

CHAPTER TWO

Picture Clues

"A Picture is Worth a Thousand Words"

You are now ready to set the stage for literacy. Children need to learn how language works, that the words on the page match spoken words, and that the pictures in the story are there to explain or add to the story.

Before you begin reading a book together look over the cover. Talk about what is pictured on the cover. Speak to your child in whole sentences. Ask questions that require more than a yes or no answer. Usually questions that start with the words who, what, where, when, why or how, will require children to think about their answer. Ask questions like "How do you know that?" and "Where in the picture do you see that?"

If you are beginning with young children you will start by pointing to each thing in the picture and naming it, using complete sentences. Do each item separately before going on to the next. Looking at a picture of some fruit you could ask questions like: "This is an apple. What is this? What color is it? What does it do? What shape is it? How is it like this orange? What do we do with apples? Where do apples grow?" You will need to adjust your questioning to suit your child's language development and attention span.

If he doesn't know what the words, "shape" or "color" mean, start by saying "The apple is red. What color is it?" In this way you are building basic concepts of size, shape and direction at the same time as developing patterns of questions.

If your child is a little older, look at the picture on the cover and inside the book. Ask about how the things and people in the pictures relate to each other. For example if the picture shows a family sitting at a holiday table eating dinner, ask questions like the following.

- What are these people doing?
- Do you think they know each other? Why?
- Who is the oldest? Youngest?
- What are they eating?
- Is it a special meal? What clues in the picture tell you that?
- What holiday do you think it is? How do you know?
- What country do you think they could live in? Why?

Ask questions to relate what is in the picture to your child's own life, to get an idea of what the story is probably about before beginning to read.

It is extremely important that you allow your child to discover as much information as possible. Of course, if he does not know anything about other cultures or customs this is a good time to tell him about them. Do not do this in excess. Monitor your child's interest and if he seems to be getting bored or impatient move ahead.

One other thing that you can do is to have a piece of paper between you, and as he names various things in the pictures write down the words. Make sure he can see you. When your questioning is over, read the words to him and ask him to repeat them. Say, "When we read the story let's see how many of these words the author used to write the story." This step is to be used with previewing and predicting which are described in Chapter Three.

Summary

1) Talk about the pictures on the cover.

2) Use complete sentences.

3) Teach the language for color, shape, size.

4) Look at the pictures in the book and talk about them.

5) Ask questions that need more than a yes or no answer.

6) Use the pictures to set the stage for the story.

Think about what you have learned so far. Were your predictions correct? How many of these ideas have you started using already? Try to add a new one as you read just to see how it feels. Now, predict what will be in the next chapter. Read on to see what you can find out!

CHAPTER THREE

Previewing and Predicting

"You Can't Judge a Book By It's Cover, Or Can You?"

When you pick up a book or magazine to read, you automatically preview and predict. This happens when you look over the book, think about what it's about, think about what you know about the topic, ask yourself if it is interesting, and if you will be able to understand the book with the information that you already have. You then make your decision to read it or not, depending on your answers. This is previewing and predicting. People who do not read well do not automatically do this. They tend just to start at page one and read. Usually the unsuccessful reader will become discouraged and give up. When you go through the process of looking over the book, asking yourself questions, relating the book to what you already know, and deciding on a reason for reading the book, you are preparing for a successful reading experience. Even before starting to read you have some idea of what is in the book. You can also probably guess at some of the information that will be in the reading. This helps you to read and understand the book more easily.

You can teach these important techniques to your children. They are simple, once you try them. The purpose of starting early is so that your child will begin to think in this way and be able to read without help.

1. Look over the book before beginning to read. Read the title and the author's name to your child. Talk about what the title might mean.

2. Talk about other books written by the same author that you have read.

3. Look over the pages and pictures inside the book. Ask your child to guess what the story will be about. Ask questions like:

   What do you think this story will be about?

   Who do you think will be in the story?

   What do you see in the pictures that tells you that?

4. Introduce the characters by saying something like, "This story is about two bears that are friends. What do you think they will do? What kinds of things do you do with your friends? Where do you think the bears will play?"

The reason for these questions is to involve your child with the ideas in the story as much as possible before actually reading.

You can test this by trying a story without this method and then another story with it. You will find that when you do use it, your child has more interest, understanding and memory of the story. You are guaranteeing a successful reading experience. Nothing succeeds like success.

As you read through the book ask questions like "What do you think will happen next? What has happened that makes you think that? Has the bear acted like that before? How do you think the boy felt when his dog ran away?" Questions that ask your child to think about why something happened or how someone felt, etc., are actively involving her in thinking and the reading process. You want your child to be actively, thoughtfully involved all the time with her environment. These strategies help with reading and can help to counteract some of the damage of passive television watching.

For example, I used these strategies with a group of five, second grade students who were supposed to repeat the first grade reading book because they had failed the test. How sad! To be a failure at six and seven years old!

I sat down with them with a book about a frog and a toad. I said "Look at the cover. What do you think the story will be about?" They looked at me with blank faces as if I was a commercial for laundry detergent and one boy shrugged and said "I don't know." I led them through the questions of: "What do you see? How do you know which one is the frog? What do their faces look like? Are they happy? Do you think they are brothers? Oh, you think they are friends. What do friends do? Do you have friends? How do you know someone is your friend?" I continued this discussion until everyone was actively involved. It was clear to me that these children had already developed the habit of not thinking. These strategies worked wonders for them and they improved dramatically over the course of the year. If they had been prepared in this way before school, they would not have had to suffer failure at such a young age.

Children are naturally curious about their environment and the people around them. They ask "Why?" all of the time. All people need a reason, or a purpose, for the things they do.

Children need a reason to read. When you are reading with your child it is important to create a "why" for them that means something to them. Saying that they need to read to do well in school is fine but not immediate enough for children. They will sit down and read with you for your attention and encouragement. If you make the experience fun, your child will become an avid reader.

After previewing, and predicting, you need to create a reason for reading the story. Usually you can use one of your child's predictions by saying, "Let's read the story now and see if these bears play the same games as you do." You can use any statement like this that can be answered in the reading. Although these purposes may not seem very important to us, children take the content of stories very seriously. Reading to see if their predictions are in the story is very motivating.

Summary

1) Preview the title, cover and pictures of a book before beginning to read.

2) Ask your child to guess what might happen in the story before reading.

3) Ask questions that need more than a yes or no answer. Encourage your child to explain how he got his answer.

4) Relate the topic and events in the story to experiences in your child's life.

5) Ask "why" frequently. Encourage risk-taking.

6) If you show interest in reading, your child will also.

7) Listen to your child's ideas. Treat them with respect.

What did you learn from this chapter? You may find that your own reading ability is starting to change by using these steps. Think about what you have read so far. Try predicting what the next chapter could be about. Ready? Read on!

CHAPTER FOUR

Reading Aloud

"Where You Lead, I Will Follow"

Now you are ready to begin reading! Start by reading the book to your child. The first time you read, it will be to see what happened in the story and if your guesses were correct. Read a whole page aloud, pointing to the words in a flowing motion as you read. Make sure that your child is looking at the words as you read them. Read in a natural voice. Remember to read slowly enough for understanding but fast enough to prevent boredom. Read the whole story this way, occasionally pausing to comment on the predictions he had made or to ask him what might happen next.

The second time you read the book it will be to have your child "read" with you. This time you will say, "Let's read this together. I will read some of the words, and you will read some of the words." Begin reading, pausing at easy-to-guess words (predictable words).

For example, "The boy was reading the b____ ." Encourage your child to guess the word. Guide him by reminding him of what the story is about, the way the sentence is written, the picture clues and the first letters in the word.

If your child guesses a word that makes sense but is not the word on the page, say "It could be paper but this word starts with a b or 'b-b-b' sound. Can you think of something that he could be reading that starts with 'b-b-b'?" (Make the sound of the letter, not the name). It is important to stress accuracy, but make sure that you also give as many clues as possible to help your child "discover" the word without being told the word. If you merely tell the word without allowing him to experience success, you reinforce the idea that he is inadequate. If the child is incorrect, make sure to comment on any part that is correct. Children are extremely sensitive to criticism and will become discouraged easily. So if he says "bag" instead of book, you respond by telling him that bag does begin with the "b-b-b" sound and that he could be reading a bag, but let's think of a word that sounds like look and starts with "b-b-b". Each time give more and more clues. You will want to select words for him to "guess" that are words that he understands.

If your child seems interested, go back for a third reading. This time tell your child to read along with you any words he remembers. Pause again at the easy-to-guess words, giving him clues if needed. This is not to be a frustrating or painful activity, so don't spend too much time on each word. Try three clues and then say, "Let me help you this time, next time you will remember it."

These steps can be done in one or two reading times. The next time you read this book you may want to practice the pages a few times each or as much as your child wants to. Any reading or writing activity that you do with your child must be determined by his interest level. Do not force reading on your child if he does not seem interested. Instead try to create interest with your enthusiasm and by pointing out how much he is able to do now. This will help your child to learn that reading is "talking on paper".

I recently tutored a child whose parents read to him nightly, but did not follow these steps. At the end of first grade he had not learned to read many words.

He was a talkative child and could discuss many topics, so I knew that he understood the language needed to read for first grade. When I began the step in this chapter with him, I could see the problem immediately. He was a passive listener and did not look at the words as I read to him. He was not actively involved. I would read along pausing for him to "guess" the next word. He would have no response. He could not remember what I had just read to him. He was not actively thinking about what was happening. He appeared to be passively waiting for me to tell him the word. I reread the sentence completely, asking him to fill in the blank. He was then able to do so. In the beginning he would guess a word that would make sense but had no connection to the letters on the page. Then I taught him to use the first letter or two of the word to help him. After only a few sessions he understood this process of "making meaning" in reading and became more confident.

Many times children see adults as being able to read and write without effort. For some children this becomes so intimidating they will not take the risk of trying. This also happens when the child suffers criticism or impatience from the adult reading with him. You must be careful not to allow any negative words, looks, sighs, etc., to be part of the reading experience. Make sure your child's teacher or day care worker understands this also.

Summary

1) The first time you read a book focus on what it means, and the flow of the language. Make it fun.

2) Encourage your child to guess at words, using the clues in the book.

3) Build your child's confidence by helping him to "guess" the words rather than just telling him.

4) By the third reading your child will believe he can read. Be sure to comment on improvements.

5) Do not make reading stressful. If the book is too hard, use simpler and simpler books, even picture books.

6) If you encourage risk-taking and reward effort, your child will be interested and stay interested.

7) Do not criticize or allow others to make your child feel inadequate.

Think about the information in this chapter. See if you can tell someone else what you have learned. Was this chapter what you expected? How was it different? Thinking about these questions will help you to see how much you are learning. Now, predict what the next chapter will be about. Happy reading!

CHAPTER FIVE

Reading Together

"Me and My Shadow..."

or

"Imitation is The Sincerest Form of Flattery"

After your child has learned how reading works, you will want to more fully involve her. Again, <u>you</u> will read the story first, using all of the steps you have learned so far. Then you will reread it all the way through together, your voice just a bit ahead of your child's. She will shadow you. This allows her to feel the flow of reading. In this way you also provide the word clues for her, but she is "reading". You will sometimes find that she will start to say the wrong word but will change to follow you. This step builds confidence and her belief that, "I can read". This belief is essential for success.

Read the story or section again, as a team, a few more times. If your child seems able and willing to try reading alone, encourage her to do so. Tell her that you will tell her the words she does not know. If it seems too hard after she starts reading, just pick up with the team reading again. It is fine to read and reread favorite stories many times, until <u>she</u> becomes tired of them.

The next step is reading alone! You may take turns reading to each other, or your child may read to you.

Whenever she is reading to you and comes to an unknown word, do not get stuck on "sounding it out". Instead tell her the word. Most early reading books are made up of sight words. Sight words are words that have to be recognized immediately. They usually cannot be sounded out. By focusing on sounding words out, you interrupt the process of reading and jeopardize understanding of the story. I have tutored many children whose beginning reading instruction focussed so much on sounding out words that they did not know the true purpose of reading: the meaning. Beginning readers need to learn letter names and sounds, but not while they are struggling to get through a first reading of a story.

After your child has read the story once, with you providing the unknown words, you can go back to those words and try sounding them out. Be careful! Many adults, no matter how they learned to read, do not know phonic patterns and rules. Also, I have even seen teachers trying to sound out sight words! It doesn't work. Instead try spelling these words for clues.

Repetition and practice are needed to learn sight words. A list of basic sight words is included at the end of this chapter. See Chapter Nine to learn how to build a word bank of sight words.

Encourage your child to read at least a few words independently every day. As her confidence grows she will want to read to you more and more. Celebrate!

It is also important to read to your child from books just for enjoyment. In this case you may not ask her to participate in the actual reading. You will read to her, asking her to picture the story in her mind. This is a good time to explain new words and ideas. Teaching your child to listen for certain things, or to make guesses or judgements about the characters, keeps her actively involved in the reading. These are important school skills, as much schoolwork involves listening and then following directions. If you can find two separate times a day to "play with" reading, you can distinguish between the time spent on learning to read, and the time spent on learning to listen. Always keep a time each day that you read to your child. Include material just above her reading level to teach her new words and ideas.

Summary

1) Model the flow of reading by reading the story to your child first.

2) "Team" read the story a few times so that your child can follow your pattern.

3) Encourage independent reading by telling your child the unknown words.

4) Make time for learning to read and learning to listen.

5) Do not focus on sounding words out.

6) Do focus on recognizing whole sight words.

7) Do focus on understanding the meaning of the story.

8) Point out to your child that she is a reader at every opportunity.

Do you understand the process of reading? If you have questions, go back and reread these chapters. Sometimes just sitting down and trying these strategies is the best way to understand them. You are teaching reading now!

Some Basic Sight Words

These are some of the basic sight words that you will find in many children's books. There are others that you may want to add to the list as you read new stories.

A	ABOUT	ABOVE	ACROSS
ADD	AFRAID	AFTER	AGAIN
AGO	AHEAD	AIR	ALL
ALONE	AN	AND	ANY
AM	ARE	AROUND	AS
ASK	ASLEEP	AT	AWAY
BAD	BAG	BE	BED
BETTER	BECAUSE	BALL	BUSH
BACK	BEGIN	BIG	BUMP
BIRTHDAY	BASKET	BEST	BUT
BY	BEFORE	BOOK	BOY
BROTHER	BEHIND	CAN	CAR
CHILDREN	CAT	COVER	COME
CHAIR	CRY	CUP	CLIMB
COLD	CLOTHES	CLOSE	COULD
DAY	DID	DO	DOG
DOWN	DARK	DISH	DOES
DOLL	DAD	DRINK	EVEN
EVER	EVERY	EVERYTHING	
EACH	END	EYE	EASY
EDGE	EARTH	EAR	EAT
EARLY	FATHER	FAT	FRIEND
FROM	FIRST	FOR	FIRE
FREE	FROG	FLY	FEEL
FACE	GIRL	GET	GIVE
GROUND	GOOD	GONE	GHOST
GARDEN	GUESS	GO	HIS
HER	HIM	HEAD	HELP
HARD	HAPPY	HAT	HERE
HEAR	HIGH	HOUSE	HOME
HOW	HE	IF	I
IDEA	IT	JUST	JAM

JAR	JUMP	KITE	KISS
KEEP	LIGHT	LITTLE	LEAVE
LET	LIKE	LAST	MORNING
MY	ME	MINE	MOTHER
MAY	MUCH	MILK	MONEY
NEW	NEXT	NO	NOT
NEVER	NOW	NOTHING	NAME
NIGHT	OF	OFF	ONLY
ONE	OPEN	OUT	OVER
OUR	OWN	ON	PLAY
PUT	PEOPLE	PARTY	PLEASE
PRESENT	PONY	PASS	PAL
QUIET	QUACK	ROOM	ROAD
REALLY	RUN	RIDE	REAL
SING	START	STREET	SWING
SHE	STAY	SAY	SAID
SISTER	SMALL	SHORT	SOME
SAW	SCARY	SANDWICH	SORRY
SILLY	SWIM	SEE	SHOUT
SAD	SIZE	SUN	SNOW
SO	SAFE	STORY	SHOULD
SECOND	STRING	STRONG	THIS
THAT	THE	THEIR	THESE
THOSE	TOAD	TABLE	TALK
THOUGHT	THINK	THERE	TODAY
TOMORROW	TAKE	TRY	TO
TOP	TIME	THEN	THEM
TREE	UNDER	UP	US
UNTIL	UPSTAIRS	USE	VERY
VAN	VET	VISIT	WATER
WERE	WENT	WANT	WANTED
WILL	WE	WAS	WITH
WORK	WASH	WISH	WET
YOU	YEAR	YELL	YES
YARD	YESTERDAY	ZOO	ZEBRA

CHAPTER SIX

Letters and Sounds and Word Families

"A is for Apple, B is for Book, C is for Cat"

You have now learned about the process of reading and various ways to help your child to become a reader. At the same time, children need to learn letter names and sounds to help them learn new words and word patterns.

Start with the letter names. First you need letters that your child can handle. You can purchase plastic or wooden letters, or make them yourself from cardboard, modeling clay, pretzel dough, sand paper, sponges or other durable material that your child can feel, trace and move. Practice one letter at a time. Begin with the letters in her name. Then go on to the rest of the consonants. Say the name of the letter, trace the shape, think of a "sample word" that represents the sound of the letter. Have your child repeat the letter name and sound.

"This letter is D. What letter is this?"

Trace the letter.

"D is for dad. D says d-d-d. What does D say?"

"Let's think of some other words that start with d-d-d."

"Dog, door, duck."

Write down the words, spelling them aloud as you write.

Three other words is enough. Attach a picture of the sample word next to the writing to help her remember the word. Put this paper up on your message board or on your refrigerator (at eye level for your child). Work on one letter a week unless your child is able to learn faster than that. Do not pressure or overload your child.

While you are working on individual letters, have an alphabet line of capital letters posted on the refrigerator. Review the line together each day. You can teach the alphabet song as you point to each letter.

"Abcd, efg, hijklmnop, qrs, tuv, wx, yz. Now I know my abc's, tell me what you think of me".

The ability to recognize a letter and to name a letter are two different skills. Letter recognition comes first. So you might say, "Point to the D", and your child will be able to do so. But if you say, "What is this letter?" and she cannot name it, do not worry. Just keep on practicing, using the "hands-on" letters to pick up, trace, and name. Continue to refer to the sample word to help identify the sound. Be sensitive with your child. Do not let learning become boring, even if you were taught that way!

After you have practiced a letter enough that your child knows it, try making a letter book. Take about five pieces of drawing paper and staple them together to make a book. Lightly draw the letter of the book twice on each page, taking about ¼ of the page. Use the capital letter and leave room for a picture. Have your child trace over your letter with a crayon or marker. With your child, look in magazines for pictures of things that start with that letter sound. Cut out the pictures and glue them next to your traced over letters. Write the word for the picture below it. Do one or two pages each day for a week.

Some Suggestions for Sample Words

B	Bed, Boy, Bird, Box, Bag
C	Cat, Car, Can
D	Dad, Dog
F	Fish, Food
G	Gum, Goat
H	Hat, House, Hen
J	Juice, Jump, Jam
K	Kangaroo
L	Lemon, Lion, Lamp, Lips
M	Man, Mom, Mouse, Money
N	Nut, Nana
P	Pet, Pillow, Popsicle, Pizza
R	Run, Rain
S	Sun, Sand
T	Toy, Table, Telephone
V	Van, Video, Vacuum, Vet
W	Water, Wax, Wiggle
X	X-ray
Y	Yellow
Z	Zoo, Zebra

Vowels (a, e, i, o, u), are more difficult to learn than consonants. Teach the long vowels first. Telling short vowel sounds apart is very difficult for many people, not just beginning readers. The best way to teach all vowels is through rhyming words (word families) that your child already understands. For each letter that you teach, provide pictures and real things to help develop the meaning and connect the letter-sound to something she already knows.

For example, for the letter "B" you could get a bag, a book and a box. Using real items to teach the sounds is effective. You can then teach a few words that rhyme with the sample word.

Use rhymes, jingles and songs to help develop the word family patterns. Play with the rhyming words to make language learning fun. Nursery rhymes, poems, jingles and silly stories all help to teach rhyming patterns. Just "playing" with these in speech is fine.

You can make up your own rhymes with your child, using real words and nonsense words. When your child has reached the point that she can read the sample word representing the letter, you can teach a word family.

Try to think of rhyming words for the sample word. Write them in a list, saying each letter as you write it. Then repeat the sample word, have your child repeat the word, and then spell it together. Ask her to tell you which letters are the same in all of the words. Tell the sound they make and read the list together.

For example, if the sample word is cat, list cat, fat, sat, and mat down the paper. Review the sound of cat. Then say "What would it say if you put "F" in the beginning?" Continue on with the rest of the words. Make up rhymes or riddles using these words.

Some Word Families

Bed	Fed	Red
Fish	Dish	Wish
Cat	Fat	Hat
Dad	Glad	Sad
Sun	Bun	Fun
House	Mouse	Blouse
Nut	Cut	Hut
Pet	Get	Let
Toy	Boy	Soy
Van	Ran	Can

These are only a few patterns but you can design your own according to your sample words.

The next step is to make a word family book. Write one word on each page. Have your child trace it, spell it, and then draw or find a picture to show its meaning.

Always make these times lighthearted, enjoyable and successful. You want your child to learn to love all aspects of communication: speaking, listening, reading, and writing. These activities will not necessarily take the place of school learning, but they will lay a good foundation. These are the kinds of things that you should look for in a beginning school program.

Summary

1) Teach one letter at a time.

2) Use things to teach the sound that goes with a letter.

3) Use letters that your child can pick up and move around to introduce the letters. Make letter books.

4) Pick a sample word for each letter and teach it as a sight word.

5) Use words rhyming with the sample words to teach word families. Make word family books.

6) Play with the sounds of words through rhymes, poems, jingles, silly songs, etc.

7) Make learning fun.

8) Practice the alphabet line every day.

Are you ready to write your own stories? Keep reading!

CHAPTER SEVEN

Beginning Writing

"A Picture is Worth a Thousand Words, Part Two"

Reading and writing work together. There are two types of writing activities for you to do with your child. There are the stories your child writes without your "help" and there are stories your child tells you that you write down.

When your child is writing his own story it is important to realize that pictures and drawings are stories too. In fact, drawing pictures is the first stage of writing. Many times your child will make marks or lines on the drawings, before he knows how to make letters. He is imitating your writing. Ask about the picture or markings. Ask what the picture is about, who is in it, what's happening. Always try to make sense of the story. Attempts at writing show that your child has the idea that writing makes meaning. As in reading, never criticize your child's pictures or writings. Focus on the meaning of the writing, not the spelling or handwriting.

Set up a writing place with different types of markers, pencils and crayons. Provide different sizes, colors and shapes of paper. Provide some books for ideas and a picture dictionary. Sit down and write with him.

Send him letters. Encourage writing to relatives or other friends. Make homemade invitations and birthday cards. Do anything you can think of to show your child that writing is enjoyable, valuable, and part of everyday life.

Many parents are concerned that their children do not use adult spelling when they are learning to write stories. Children learn to spell in stages, usually like this:

1. One letter over and over.
2. More than one letter to represent a word.
3. Some letters that are sounds in the word.
4. Beginning consonant sounds.
5. Other consonant sounds.
6. Other consonant sounds in the right places.
7. Vowels, but maybe not the right ones.
8. More regular spellings.

Do not expect to see too much regular, correct spelling until the end of second grade. If too much emphasis is placed on this, children learn that what is valuable is not their ideas, but how they spell. As a result, if they cannot yet spell like adults, they will be discouraged from writing. You can learn much about your child from his stories.

There are many adults, including teachers, who avoid writing, even hate it! That is because they learned that what was important was "how" they wrote, not "what" they wrote.

You can take your child's stories and combine them into little books that he can read to friends and family. If you cannot read what he has written, ask him to read it to you. Do not be concerned if he does not read it the same way every time, especially in the early years.

Summary

1) Drawings and making marks on a paper are the first steps in writing.

2) Talk to your child about his pictures to "discover" his story.

3) Ask questions to find more details.

4) As your child begins making letters to go with his pictures, do not criticize spelling or handwriting.

5) Create a writing place with many different types of paper and writing utensils.

6) Make little books out of the drawings and writings to share with others.

7) Do not be concerned if he does not remember his story the same way it is written every time.

8) Do not be concerned about regular spelling until the end of second grade.

You have set the stage for literacy in your child's life. Good work!

CHAPTER EIGHT

Dictated Stories

"Tell Me a Story, Please"

Dictated stories is an activity that I have used with children of all ages if they have not yet learned to read. This is not to be used in place of your own child's writing, as you want her to believe that her own writing is fine. This is a team writing activity. Tell your child that the two of you are going to write a story together. Say that you will be the secretary and she will tell you the story.

You will need lined paper, pencil, marker, index cards and materials to make a little book. First, sit down with your child at a table or desk, sitting so that you can write and she can see the words as you write them. Talk about an idea or experience to write a story about. You can get some ideas from after school activities, playing with friends, going to the store, etc. Ask questions beginning with the words who, what, where, when, why, and how, to get some ideas flowing. Tell her that you will be the secretary as long as she looks at the words as you write the story that she is telling you.

Now ask, "How would you like to start your story?" Write down the story exactly as she says it. Do not change the wording, because when she "reads" it back to you, she is going to use her own words, not yours. Spell correctly and use punctuation.

If you find that your child uses poor grammar, repeat the idea back to her correctly, and then ask "What do you want me to write now?" Sometimes she will chose the correct form, but if not, write down what she says.

An example of this is: Tomorrow we went to the store. Your response would be to ask if she had gone to the store already. If she said yes, then you would say, "Do you mean yesterday we went to the store?" Other common examples are incorrect tenses and pronouns, and using the word <u>and</u> to start every sentence. If you find that your child is using poor grammar frequently, you need to reflect on how you and others speak to her, as children learn language by imitation. Make sure to model correct language patterns and speak in whole sentences whenever you speak to your child, but do not focus too much on this when working on dictated stories.

Continue to write what she says, reading the entire story with her every couple of sentences. If she seems to have said all that she has to say, ask "Do you have more to add to the story?" If not, re-read the whole story together, pointing to each word as you read. Do not be surprised if she cannot remember the beginning. Reread it two more times together.

Ask your child to circle three words in the story that she would like to learn to read. Use a pencil. If she says that she knows them all, pick three yourself that you know she does not know. You can say that although she feels that she knows them, you would like to practice them a little more just to be sure.

Darken the periods or other punctuation. Together count how many sentences there are by following the lines with your finger to the next period. Many children entering second grade do not know what a sentence is. After you have determined how many sentences there are, ask her to give a name to the story. Write the title at the beginning.

Take the first index card. On the blank side write the first circled word by asking your child to spell it to you. After you have written it, tell her the word and spell it together. Now, turn the card over and ask her to read you the sentence from the story that contains the circled word, as you write it down. You will probably have to start reading the sentence together. Underline the circled word in the sentence. Flip the card over and ask her to read it. If she cannot remember the word, turn the card over and read the sentence. Flip the card back to the front for her to say the word. Practice this a few more times. Repeat these steps for the other two words.

Combine the three words into a pack, along with any cards from previous stories and practice flashing them. If she does not know the word, try cuing her with the first sound of the word. If that does not work, then turn the card over and read the sentence. Practice these words everyday. If you make a game out of it, it will be fun.

Finally, reread the story one more time. Ask her to try reading it alone with the condition that you will help with the words that she does not know.

This is a good time to have her read the story to you as you either type it, or neatly write it, into a little book. Leave enough room for her to draw pictures to go with the story (one sentence on each page). These stories can be done every two or three days. Do not go ahead until your child has learned at least two of the words. If she is having difficulty, pick easier words. Sometimes I include words that they already know to ensure some success. You can practice the word cards in between stories.

These stories can be read to other family members, sent to grandparents, placed in the family library, and taken to school. Be extremely positive throughout this process. Praise and encourage everything she does know. Do not comment on what she does not know. Children who have had difficulty learning to read need extra attention and praise.

Summary

1) Encourage your child to write her own stories, separate from dictated stories.

2) Begin by talking about experiences.

3) Have your child dictate a story to you. Use your child's language exactly as it is said to you.

4) Become aware of the speech patterns you are teaching your child.

5) Team read the story together a few times.

6) Have your child select three words to learn to read.

7) Write the words on word cards and the sentence containing each word on the back of each card.

8) Practice flash reading the words, using the sentence on the back of the card for clues.

9) Have your child read the story to you as you type or write it into a little book to be illustrated.

10) Practice the word cards and rereading the story a few times.

11) Write a new story every few days or when the word cards are learned.

12) Provide opportunities for your child to share these stories with others.

This step can be done with all children or you can skip ahead to the next chapter. What do you think the next chapter is about? If you said word banks, you are right!

CHAPTER NINE

Building a Word Bank

"A Penny Saved is a Penny Earned"

Building a word bank is a form of saving. It is a collection of words on index cards that your child learns to read at sight. These can be taken from dictated stories or from team reading stories. As the number of cards grows your child can see his success growing too, just as in a savings account. Building a word bank is necessary as a foundation for beginning reading.

Your child's word bank can be in an index box, or a covered container large enough to hold the cards. You do not have to use full size index cards. Just make sure that the print is large and your child can see it without problems. This is an opportunity to have fun and be creative. You can use and decorate many different types of containers, or use ribbon or rubber bands to hold the cards together. Also you can cut different shapes out of the cards to create interest. This will be your child's bank so make sure to involve him as much as possible in all of these decisions.

The process is similar to that of dictated stories, except in this case you will use books by other authors. You can advance to this step after dictated stories and combine your word banks.

The steps are listed below.

1) Select a story with your child that is interesting to him. Start with easy books that have short sentences.

2) Go through the process of previewing and predicting.

3) Read the story to him.

4) Reread the story using the reading aloud process or the team reading process.

5) After you have read the story a few times, ask him to choose a word from each page that he would like to learn to read. Proceed one page at a time and no more than three words in a session.

6) Have him spell the first word to you (from the book) as you write it on the blank side of an index card.

7) Turn the card over and have him read the sentence containing the circled word to you, as you write it down. You will probably have to read the sentence together. Underline the circled word.

8) Flash the word card to him. If he does not know the word, turn the card over and read the sentence together. Then flash the card again. Practice a few times. Then go on to the next word. When your child has read a word without assistance for five days in a row, you can give it a rest for a few weeks. Just make sure to periodically review all of the words. If you find that he has forgotten a word, add it to the current pack.

9) Add three to five words at a time. Make sure not to pressure or overwhelm him.

10) Practice these words every day. Your child may need to draw pictures on the card to help him remember. This is fine. These word cards can be used to play games like concentration (you need a double set), rhyming games or putting words together to make sentences. You can take a few of them that make sentences and put them in an envelope. Then "send" it to him as a message. He will have to read the cards and rearrange them to get the message.

Make sure to talk about the meaning of the words. Use them in sentences. Have your child use them in oral sentences. Talk about what they mean in the story. When you have a bundle of words, you can start talking about words that mean the same thing, or words that are in the same group.

For example, if you have the words chair, table, bed and sink, you can discuss what they have in common (they are furniture, what they are used for, what room they are usually found in).

This is another opportunity to be creative with practicing the words. Try not to let it be a boring experience. Make sure to praise all advances. Let your child know that you are proud of him for each new word he learns. Once he becomes a fluent reader, you will not need the word bank any more.

Summary

1) A sight word bank is the foundation of beginning reading.

2) Be creative with the size, shape and container of the word cards.

3) Select an easy story without too many words to start.

4) Follow the process for reading aloud or team reading.

5) Have your child select one word on each page to learn.

6) Prepare the word cards.

7) Practice the word cards daily in creative and fun ways.

8) Practice reading the story until your child can read most of it.

9) Move on to a new story every four or five days if your child is ready.

10) Point out and praise the learning of new words.

You have done a fine job! You are truly your child's first teacher.

CHAPTER TEN

Reading Success For Children

"You are Truly Your Child's First Teacher"

As you have found from reading this book, parents have the power to make a tremendous difference in their children's education. The children with the most successful school experiences come from homes in which literacy is valued and nurtured.

Throughout this book I have stressed maintaining your child's self-confidence and a positive attitude toward learning to read and write. A child will not be successful without experiences to develop his knowledge of the world, or without someone interested enough to talk about these experiences. This language base is the root of reading and writing. This is a crucial role that you play in helping your child to develop school skills.

There are other things you can do throughout the elementary grades to promote success. Join a children's book club or buy a subscription to a children's magazine. Act out stories with your children using finger or hand puppets. Use taped stories with books (talking books) with your child for an independent activity or on a long car trip. Sing songs, recite poems and jingles, tell stories and jokes, play games, do puzzles, and talk together.

Limit the quantity and quality of television watching. Make up a basket of activities to do instead of watching television. Take time for your children. Not just to be in the same room, but to talk, play, read, and write. Make sure that your children eat nutritionally, sleep enough and get enough exercise.

Monitor your children's school experiences. Speak up if you do not like, or do not understand, what is happening. It is your right to protect your children. If your children's school does not welcome you, find another one.

Encourage and praise your children daily. Do not criticize or be sarcastic with them. Set reasonable limits and help your children understand them.

In the past fifteen years, as a Reading Specialist, I have instructed students and teachers in kindergarten through eighth grade. I have had the opportunity to teach many older students how to read. I feel confident that if their parents knew what you now know, these students would have experienced much more success at an earlier age.

I have worked with hundreds of beginning readers and students in grades two through five who have had difficulty learning to read. I have used the steps described in this book with great success. I believe that just reading to a child is not sufficient preparation for school reading and writing success. I know these strategies will work as well for you as they have for my students. I welcome your comments and suggestions. Write to me at Learning Strategies, Box 709, Rye Beach, NH 03871.

Recommended Authors

This is a list of authors that I have enjoyed with children. There are many other fine authors for you to chose from. This list is a place to start. These authors may have other titles not listed here so be sure to check for the author's name, not just the title.

Aardema, Verna
Why Mosquitoes Buzz in People's Ears
Who's In The Rabbit's House
Tales From The Story Hat

Allard, Harry
Miss Nelson Is Missing!
Miss Nelson Has A Field Day
Miss Nelson Is Back
It's So Nice To Have A Wolf Around The House

Andersen, Hans Christian
The Emperor's New Clothes
The Fir Tree
The Little Match Girl
The Nightingale
The Little Mermaid
The Princess And The Pea
The Snow Queen
Thumbelina
The Ugly Duckling

Anno, Mitsumasa
Anno's Alphabet
Anno's Counting Book
Anno's Counting House
Anno's Hat Tricks

Bang, Molly
The Grey Lady And The Strawberry Snatcher
Dawn
Ten, Nine, Eight
Wiley And The Hairy Man
The Paper Crane
Yellow Ball

Barrett, Judy
Animals Should Definitely Not Wear Clothing
I Hate To Go To Bed
I Hate To Take A Bath

Bemelmans, Ludwig
Madeline
Madeline's Rescue

Bond, Michael
A Bear Called Paddington
More About Paddington
Paddington At Large
Paddington Helps Out
Paddington Marches On
Paddington Takes Air

Brown, Marc
Arthur's Pet Business
Finger Rhymes
Hand Rhymes
Arthur's Nose
Arthur's Eyes
Arthur's Tooth
Arthur's Halloween

Brown, Marcia
The Bun: A Tale From Russia
Dick Whittington And His Cat
The Flying Carpet
The Neighbors
Stone Soup
The Blue Jackal
Henry — Fisherman
Once A Mouse
All Butterflies
Cinderella

Brown, Margaret Wise
Goodnight Moon!
The Little Fir Tree
The Little Fur Family
The Runaway Bunny
Christmas In The Barn
The Dead Bird
The Sleepy Little Lion
Brer Rabbit: Stories From Uncle Remus

Brothers, Grimm — Various illustrators have differing versions of these stories.
The Donkey Prince
The Frog Prince
Grimm's Fairy Tales
Hansel and Gretel
Little Red Riding Hood
Rapunzel
Rumpelstilskin
The Shoemaker And The Elves
The Sleeping Beauty
Snow White And The Seven Dwarfs
Tom Thumb
The Traveling Musicians

Burton, Virginia Lee
The Little House
Mike Mulligan And His Steam Shovel

Carle, Eric
The Very Quiet Cricket
The Very Hungry Caterpillar
Pancakes, Pancakes
Do You Want To Be My Friend?
The Mixed Up Chameleon
The Very Busy Spider
The Grouchy Lady Bug
The Secret Birthday Message

Cohen, Miriam
Best Friends
The New Teacher
When Will I Read?
Will I Have A Friend?

Conford, Ellen
Eugene The Brave
Impossible The Possum
Just The Thing For Geraldine

Cooney, Barbara
Chanticleer And The Fox
Miss Rumphius

DeAngeli, Marguerite
The Book Of Nursery And Mother Goose Rhymes
The Goose Girl
The Door In The Wall

DeBrunhoff, Jean
The Story of Babar

DePaola, Tomi
Nana Upstairs And Nana Downstairs
Tomi DePaola's Mother Goose
Big Anthony And The Magic Ring
Bonjour Mr. Satie
Strega Nona
Strega Nona's Magic Lessons
Helga's Dowry: A Troll Love Story

Duvoisin, Roger
Petunia
The Three Sneezes And Other Swiss Tales

Ets, Marie Hall
Gilberto And The Wind
Play With Me

Frasconi, Antonio
The House That Jack Built
See Again, Say Again

Freeman, Don
Corduroy
A Pocket For Corduroy
Dandelion
Inspector Peckit

Gág, Wanda
Millions Of Cats
The ABC Bunny
Nothing At All
Gone Is Gone

Galdone, Paul
Little Red Riding Hood
The Teeny-Tiny Woman
The Three Billy Goats Gruff
The History Of Simple Simon
The House That Jack Built

Old Mother Hubbard And Her Dog
Henny, Penny
The Little Red Hen
The Old Woman And Her Pig
The Three Wishes
Tom, Tom, The Piper's Son
The Three Bears
The Three Little Pigs
Androcles And The Lion
The Monkey And The Crocodile
The Town Mouse And The Country Mouse

Gannett, Ruth Stiles

My Father's Dragon
Elmer And The Dragon
The Dragons Of Blueland

Greenaway, Kate

Mother Goose, Or The Old Nursery Rhymes
A - Apple Pie

Hoban, Russell

Bedtime For Frances
Bread And Jam For Frances
Best Friends For Frances
A Baby Sister For Frances
A Bargain For Frances
A Birthday For Frances

Hoban, Tanya

Big Ones, Little Ones
Count And See
Look Again!

Hutchins, Pat

Good-Night Owl!
Rosie's Walk
The Surprise Party
Titch

Keats, Ezra Jack
The Snowy Day
Cat Goes Fiddle-I-Fee
Peter's Chair
Whistle For Willie
Over In The Meadow
Dreams
Goggles
Hi, Cat!
A Letter To Amy
Pet Show!
John Henry, An American Legend

Kipling, Rudyard
The Elephant's Child
How The Leopard Got His Spots
How The Rhinocerous Got His Skin
Just So Stories

Kraus, Robert
Leo The Late Bloomer
Milton The Early Riser
Owliver

Krauss, Ruth
The Carrot Seed
The Backward Day
A Very Special House

Kunhardt, Dorothy
Pat The Bunny

Lenski, Lois
Cowboy Small
Policeman Small

Lindgren, Astrid
Pippi Goes On Board
Pippi In The South Seas

Pippi Longstocking
Pippi On The Run

Lionni, Leo
Swimmy
Inch By Inch
Frederick's Fables: A Leo Lionni Treasury of
    Favorite Stories
The Biggest House In The World
Fish Is Fish
Alexander And The Wind-Up Mouse
Federick
Little Blue And Little Yellow
Tico And The Golden Wings

Lobel, Arnold
Frog And Toad Together
Frog And Toad Are Friends
Days With Frog And Toad
Mouse Tales
Whiskers And Rhymes
Ming Lo Moves The Mountain
The Random House Book Of Poetry For Children
The Very Tall Mouse And The Very Short Mouse
On The Day Peter Stuyvesant Sailed Into Town
Owl At Home

Martin, Bill, Jr.
Brown Bear, Brown Bear, What Do You See?
Martin, Bill, Jr., and John Archambault
Listen To The Rain
The Ghost-Eye Tree
Up And Down On The Merry-Go-Round
Barnyard Dance

Mayer, Mercer
There's A Nightmare In My Closet
Frog Goes To Dinner
A Boy, A Dog And A Frog

Ah-Choo
One Frog Too Many
Hiccup
Oops
If I Had . . .
Frog, Where Are You?

McCloskey, Robert
Make Way For Ducklings
Blueberries For Sal
One Morning In Maine

McPhail, David
First Flight
Fix It
Emma's Pet
Emma's Vacation
The Train
The Bear's Toothache

Milne, A.A.
Winnie-The-Pooh
The House At Pooh Corner

Minarik, Else Holmelund
Little Bear
Little Bear's Visit
Father Bear Comes Home
A Kiss For Little Bear
Little Bear's Friend
The Little Girl And The Dragon
It's Spring

Oxenbury, Helen
Pig Tale
Helen Oxenbury's ABC Of Things
Numbers Of Things

Parish, Peggy
Amelia Bedelia
Come Back, Amelia Bedelia
Good Work, Amelia Bedelia
Amelia Bedelia And The Baby
Amelia Bedelia Goes Camping
Merry Christmas, Amelia Bedelia
Amelia Bedelia And The Surprise Shower
Play Ball, Amelia Bedelia
Thank You, Amelia Bedelia
Too Many Rabbits
The Costume Party

Piper, Watty
The Little Engine That Could

Potter, Beatrix
The Tale Of Peter Rabbit
The Tale Of Benjamin Bunny
The Tale Of Squirrel Nutkin
The Tale Of Mrs. Tiggy-Winkle
The Tale Of Tom Kitten
The Tale Of Jemima Puddleduck

Preston, Edna Mitchell
Squawk To The Moon, Little Goose
The Temper Tantrum Book
Where Did My Mother Go?

Rockwell, Anne
The Three Bears And 15 Other Stories

Schwartz, Alvin
In A Dark, Dark Room
Scary Stories To Tell In The Dark: Collected From American Folklore
More Scary Stories To Tell In The Dark, Too

Sendak, Maurice
Where The Wild Things Are
Alligators All Around: An Alphabet
Chicken Soup With Rice: A Book Of Months
One Was Johnny: A Counting Book
In The Night Kitchen
The Nutshell Library
Pierre

Slobodkina, Esphyr
Caps For Sale

Spier, Peter
Crash! Bang! Boom!
To Market, To Market
London Bridge Is Falling Down
Gobble Growl Grunt
Noah's Ark

Steig, William
Amos And Boris
Roland And The Minstrel Pig
Sylvester And The Magic Pebble
The Amazing Bone
Caleb And Kate

Dr. Suess, pseud. (Theodor S. Geisel)
The Cat In The Hat
One Fish, Two Fish, Red Fish, Blue Fish
And To Think That I Saw It On Mulberry Street
Horton Hatches The Egg
McElligot's Pool
Green Eggs And Ham
The 500 Hats of Bartholomew Cubbins
Bartholomew And The Oobleck
Thidwick, The Big-Hearted Moose

Tudor, Tasha
Mother Goose

A Is For Annabelle
1 Is One

Leeuwen, Jean Van
Amanda Pig And Her Big Brother Oliver
Tales Of Oliver Pig
More Tales Of Oliver Pig
More Tales Of Amanda Pig

Viorst, Judith
Alexander And The Terrible, Horrible, No Good,
    Very Bad Day
Alexander, Who Used To Be Rich Last Sunday
I'll Fix Anthony
The Tenth Good Thing About Barney

Waber, Bernard
Ira Sleeps Over
The House On East 88th Street
"You Look Ridiculous," Said The Rhinocerous To
    The Hippopotamus

Walters, Marguerite
The City-Country ABC

Ward, Lynd
The Biggest Bear
The Silver Pony

Wells, Rosemary
Noisy Nora

Wilder, Laura Ingalls
Little House In The Big Woods
Farmer Boy
Little House On The Prairie
On The Banks Of Plum Creek
By The Shores Of Silver Lake
The Long Winter

*The Little House Cookbook: Frontier Foods From
    Laura Ingalls Wilder's Classic Stories*
Little Town On The Prairie
These Happy Golden Years

Yashima, Taro, pseud. (Jun Iwamatsu)
Crow Boy
Seashore Story
Umbrella
The Village Tree
Youngest One

Zemach, Harve
Duffy And The Devil
Nail Soup

Zemach, Margot
The Three Sillies
It Could Always Be Worse

Zolotow, Charlotte
William's Doll
Mr. Rabbit And The Lovely Present
Do You Know What I'll Do?
A Father Like That
The Hating Book
If It Weren't For You
Big Brother
My Friend John
The Quarreling Book
Big Sister And Little Sister

Caldecott Medal Books

The Caldecott Medal, is given each year to the illustrator of the "most distinguished" American picture book, by the Association for Library Service to Children.

1998 **Rapunzel**
Paul O. Zelinsky

1997 **Golem**
David Wisniewski

1996 **Officer Buckle and Gloria**
Peggy Rathmann

1995 **Smoky Night**
David Diaz

1994 **Grandfather's Journey**
Allen Say

1993 **Mirette on the High Wire**
Emily Arnold McCully

1992 **Tuesday**
David Wiesner

1991 **Black and White**
David Macaulay

1990 **Lon Po Po: A Red Riding Hood Story from China**
Ed Young

1989 **Song and Dance Man**
Karen Ackerman

1988 **Owl Moon**
Jane Yolen

1987 **Hey, Al**
Arthur Yorinks

1986 **The Polar Express**
Chris Van Allsburg

1985 **Saint George and the Dragon**
Margaret Hodges

1984 **The Glorious Flight: Across the Channel
with Louis Bleriot**
Alice and Martin Provensen

1983 **Shadow**
Blaise Cendrars

1982 **Jumanji**
Chris Van Allsburg

1981 **Fables**
Arnold Lobel

1980 **Ox-Cart Man**
Donald Hall

1979 **The Girl Who Loved Wild Horses**
Paul Goble

1978 **Noah's Ark**
Peter Spier

1977 **Ashanti to Zulu: African Traditions**
Margaret Musgrove

1976 **Why Mosquitoes Buzz in People's Ears**
Verna Aardema

1975 **Arrow to the Sun**
Gerald McDermott

1974 **Duffy and the Devil**
Harve Zemach

1973 **The Funny Little Woman**
Arlene Mosel

1972 **One Fine Day**
Nonny Hogrogian

1971 **A Story A Story**
Gail E. Haley

1970 **Sylvester and the Magic Pebble**
William Steig

1969 **The Fool of the World and the Flying Ship**
Arthur Ransume

1968 **Drummer Hoff**
Barbara Emberley

1967 **Sam, Bangs & Moonshine**
Evaline Ness

1966 **Always Room for One More**
Sorche Nic Leodhas

1965   **May I Bring a Friend?**
Beatrice Schenk de Regniers

1964   **Where the Wild Things Are**
Maurice Sendak

1963   **The Snowy Day**
Ezra Jack Keats

1962   **Once A Mouse**
Marcia Brown

1961   **Baboushka and the Three Kings**
Ruth Robbins

1960   **Nine Days to Christmas**
Marie Hall Ets and Aurora Labastida

1959   **Chanticleer and the Fox**
Barbara Cooney

1958   **Time of Wonder**
Robert McCloskey

1957   **A Tree is Nice**
Janice Udry

1956   **Frog Went A-Courtin'**
John Langstaff

1955   **Cinderella**
Marcia Brown

1954   **Madeline's Rescue**
Ludwig Bemelmans

1953   **The Biggest Bear**
Lynd Ward

1952   **Finders Keepers**
Will Lipkind

1951   **The Egg Tree**
Katherine Milhous

1950   **Song of the Swallows**
Leo Politi

1949   **The Big Snow**
Berta and Elmer Hader

1948   **White Snow, Bright Snow**
Alvin Tresselt

Newbery Award Winners

The Newbery Award is given each year to the author of the "most distinguished" piece of American childrens' literature.

1998 **Out of the Dust**
Karen Hesse
1997 **The View from Saturday**
E.L. Konigsburg
1996 **The Midwife's Apprentice**
Karen Cushman
1995 **Walk Two Moons**
Sharon Creech
1994 **The Giver**
Lois Lowry
1993 **Missing May**
Cynthia Rylant
1992 **Shiloh**
Phyllis Reynolds
1991 **Maniac Magee**
Jerry Spinelli
1990 **Number the Stars**
Lois Lowry
1989 **Joyful Noise: Poems for Two Voices**
Paul Fleischman
1988 **Lincoln: A Photobiography**
Russell Freedman
1987 **The Whipping Boy**
Sid Fleischman
1986 **Sarah, Plain and Tall**
Patricia MacLachlan
1985 **The Hero and the Crown**
Robin McKinley

1984   **Dear Mr. Henshaw**
        Beverly Cleary

1983   **Dicey's Song**
        Cynthia Voigt

1982   **A Visit to William Bake's Inn: Poems for
        Innocent and Experienced Travelers**
        Nancy Willard

1981   **Jacob Have I Loved**
        Katherine Paterson

1980   **A Gathering of Days**
        Joan W. Blos

1979   **The Westing Game**
        Ellen Raskin

1978   **Bridge to Terabithia**
        Katherine Paterson

1977   **Roll of Thunder, Hear My Cry**
        Mildred D. Taylor

1976   **The Grey King**
        Susan Cooper

1975   **M.C. Higgins, the Great**
        Virginia Hamilton

1974   **The Slave Dancer**
        Paula Fox

1973   **Julie of the Wolves**
        Jean Craighead George

1972   **Mrs. Frisby and the Rats of NIMB**
        Robert C. O'Brien

1971   **Summer of the Swans**
        Betsy Byars

1970   **Sounder**
        William H. Armstrong

1969   **The High King**
        Lloyd Alexander

1968   **From the Mixed-Up Files of
        Mrs. Basil E. Frankweiler**
        E.L. Koningsburg

1967   **Up a Road Slowly**
        Irene Hunt

BIBLIOGRAPHY

References and Suggested Readings

Clay, Marie M., "Reading: The Patterning of Complex Behavior", Heineman Educational Books, Auckland, 1979.

Clay, Marie M., "The Early Detection of Reading Difficulties: A Diagnostic Survey with Recovery Procedures", Heinemann Educational Books, Auckland, 1979.

Cochrane, Orin; Cochrane, Donna; Scalena, Sharen; Buchanan, Ethel, "Reading, Writing and Caring", Whole Language Consultants, Ltd., Winnipeg, 1984.

Goodman, Frank, "What's Whole in Whole Language?", Heineman, Portsmouth, NH, 1986.

Graves, Donald, "Writing: Teachers and Children at Work", Heineman, Portsmouth, NH, 1982.

Hansen, Jane, "When Writers Read", Heineman, Portsmouth, NH, 1987.

Johnson, Dale D.; Pearson, David P., "Teaching Reading Vocabulary", Holt, Rinehart and Winston, New York, 1978.

Sampson, Michael R., "The Pursuit of Literacy: Early Reading and Writing", Kendall/Hunt Publishing Company, Dubuque, 1986.

Smith, Frank, "Understanding Reading: A Psycholinguistic Analysis of Reading and Learning To Read", Holt, Rinehart and Winston, Inc., New York, 1971.

Tierney, Robert J.; Readence, John E.; Dishner, Ernest K., "Reading Strategies and Practices: A Guide for Improving Instruction", Allyn and Bacon, Inc., Boston, MA, 1980.

Index

About The Author

Joyce Corbin has been teaching children to read all her life. From her first school experience of kindergarten, when she would commandeer her siblings and friends to "teach" them after school, to the present day as a reading specialist for learning disabled children. She teaches graduate school courses, conducts teacher and parent seminars, tutors private students, and consults with school districts.

Throughout high school, in South Burlington, Vermont, where she grew up, she babysat and, unkowingly, taught reading to the children. By reading to them and asking questions, she transferred her love of reading and language to them.

During college at the University of Vermont, she continued child care and the study of reading, earning a B.S. in Education in 1975. This continued later at the University of New Hampshire, resulting in an M.Ed. specializing in Reading, in 1981.

Joyce Corbin believes that all children have the right to learn to read and experience successful happy, school years. She has learned from years of teaching older students who have failed first, that early success is the single most important job of schools and parents.

Reading Success For Children

is available by mail order

Telephone orders: Call toll free 1-800-874-READ (7323)

  Please have your Visa or Mastercard ready.

Fax orders: 603-964-2356

E-Mail orders: lrnstrat@aol.com

Postal orders: Learning Strategies, P.O. Box 709

  Rye Beach, NH 03871

Please send me _____ copies of Reading Success For Children. I am enclosing $8.95 plus $1.75 shipping and handling for **each** copy. Please make check payable to **Learning Strategies.**

Name _____

Address _____

City _____State _____ Zip _____

Payment: ☐ Check

  ☐ Visa ☐ Mastercard

Card number _____

Name on card: _____Exp. Date_____

Book total $_____

Shipping & Handling $_____

Applicable Sales Tax (CA,NJ,NY,PA) $ _____

TOTAL DUE $_____

Please allow 3-6 weeks for delivery.

Thank you!

NOTES